Copyright© 2024 Michelle Knight. All rights reserved.

All rights reserved. This book, or parts thereof, may not be reproduced in any form, stored in any retrieval system, or transmitted in any form by any means, electronic, mechanical, photocopy, recording, or otherwise, without permission of the author, except provided by the United States of America copyright law or in the case of brief quotations embodied in critical articles and reviews.

Hardback ISBN: 978-1-956911-27-5
Softback ISBN: 978-1-956911-28-2

My Feelings Matter

Speak Freely little King's

All About Me

Name: _____

Favorite Color: _____

Favorite Movie: _____

My superpower to the world is:

_____

Favorite T.V. Show: _____

Favorite Sport: _____

Favorite Sports Team: _____

Friends: _____

 **SPEAK FREELY**

Date:

Today I am grateful for:

_____

_____

Best Moment of my Day:

_____

_____

 Happiness Scale

☆ ☆ ☆ ☆ ☆

Affirmation of the Day:

I am LOVED!

 **Word of the Day:** *Generosity- Willingness to give.*

_____

_____

_____

_____

_____

_____

"My Feelings Matter"

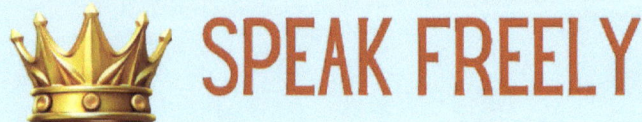 **SPEAK FREELY**

Date:

Today I am grateful for:

_____

_____

Best Moment of my Day:

_____

_____

Happiness Scale
☆ ☆ ☆ ☆ ☆

Affirmation of the Day:

I am smart.

 **"My Feelings Matter"**

_____

_____

_____

_____

_____

_____

_____

Word of the Day: Flammable- Easily ignited; burn quickly.

 **SPEAK FREELY**

Date:

Today I am grateful for:

_____

_____

Best Moment of my Day:

_____

_____

Happiness Scale

☆ ☆ ☆ ☆ ☆

Affirmation of the Day:

I am Confident!

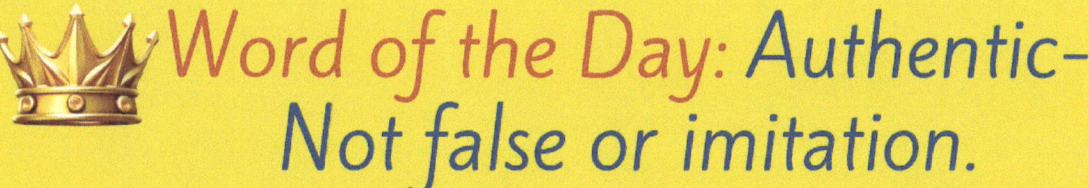 **Word of the Day:** Authentic- Not false or imitation.

_____

_____

_____

_____

_____

_____

"My Feelings Matter"

 **SPEAK FREELY**

Date:

Today I am grateful for:

_____

_____

Best Moment of my Day:

_____

_____

Happiness Scale

☆ ☆ ☆ ☆ ☆

Affirmation of the Day:
I am uniquely made!

 # "My Feelings Matter"

_____

_____

_____

_____

_____

_____

_____

Word of the Day: Tangible- Something that can be touched or felt.

 **SPEAK FREELY**

Date:

Today I am grateful for:

_____

_____

Best Moment of my Day:

_____

_____

Happiness Scale

☆ ☆ ☆ ☆ ☆

Affirmation of the Day:

It's OK to feel all my feelings!

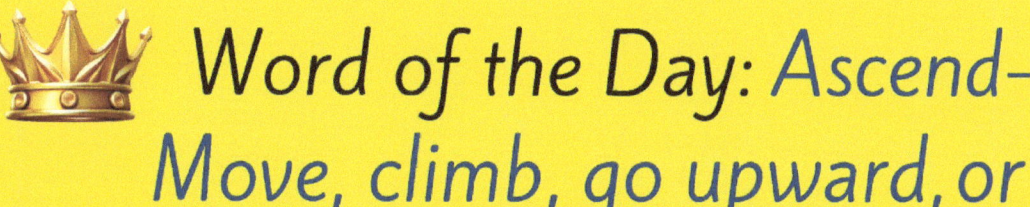 **Word of the Day: Ascend-** Move, climb, go upward, or rise.

_____

_____

_____

_____

_____

_____

"My Feelings Matter"

 **SPEAK FREELY**

 Date:

Today I am grateful for:

_____

_____

Best Moment of my Day:

_____

_____

Happiness Scale

☆ ☆ ☆ ☆ ☆

Affirmation of the Day:

I love myself!

 # "My Feelings Matter"

_____

_____

_____

_____

_____

_____

_____

**Word of the Day: Finite-
Having clear limits.**

 **SPEAK FREELY**

Date:

Today I am grateful for:

_____

_____

Best Moment of my Day:

_____

_____

 Happiness Scale

☆ ☆ ☆ ☆ ☆

Affirmation of the Day:

I have a big Heart!

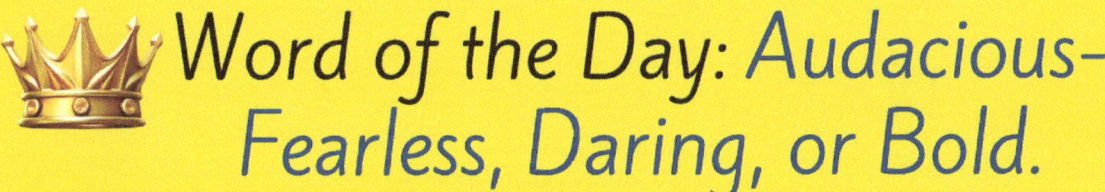 **Word of the Day: Audacious- Fearless, Daring, or Bold.**

_____

_____

_____

_____

_____

_____

_____

"My Feelings Matter"

 **SPEAK FREELY**

Date:

Today I am grateful for:

_____

_____

Best Moment of my Day:

_____

_____

Happiness Scale

☆ ☆ ☆ ☆ ☆

Affirmation of the Day:
I have manners!

# "My Feelings Matter"

_____

_____

_____

_____

_____

_____

_____

Word of the Day: Famish- Deprived of food; Starve.

Date:

Today I am grateful for:

_____

_____

Best Moment of my Day:

_____

_____

_____

Happiness Scale

☆ ☆ ☆ ☆ ☆

Affirmation of the Day:

I am not afraid of a challenge!

👑 **Word of the Day: Artificial-** Made by humans and not created naturally.

_____

_____

_____

_____

_____

_____

"My Feelings Matter"

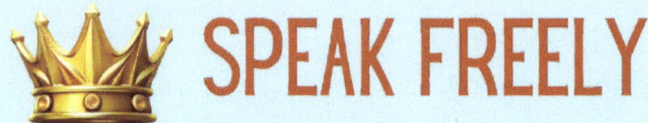 **SPEAK FREELY**

Date:

Today I am grateful for:

_____

_____

Best Moment of my Day:

_____

_____

Happiness Scale

☆ ☆ ☆ ☆ ☆

Affirmation of the Day:
I can't control other people, but I can control how I respond to them!

 # "My Feelings Matter"

_____

_____

_____

_____

_____

_____

_____

**Word of the Day: Abruptly-
Move suddenly and unexpectantly.**

 **SPEAK FREELY**

Date:

Today I am grateful for:

_____

_____

Best Moment of my Day:

_____

_____

 Happiness Scale

☆ ☆ ☆ ☆ ☆

Affirmation of the Day:

I am kind!

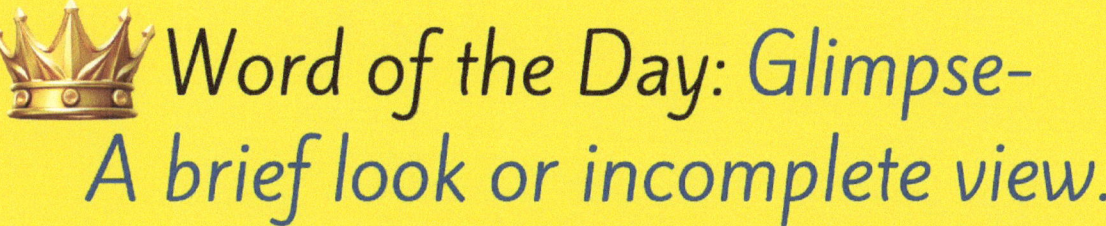 **Word of the Day: Glimpse-
A brief look or incomplete view.**

_____

_____

_____

_____

_____

_____

"My Feelings Matter"

 **SPEAK FREELY**

 Date:

Today I am grateful for:

_____

_____

Best Moment of my Day:

_____

_____

 Happiness Scale

☆ ☆ ☆ ☆ ☆

Affirmation of the Day:

I am enough!

"My Feelings Matter"

Word of the Day: Sacrifice- Giving up something you love or something valuable.

 **SPEAK FREELY**

Date:

Today I am grateful for:

_____

_____

Best Moment of my Day:

_____

_____

Happiness Scale

☆ ☆ ☆ ☆ ☆

Affirmation of the Day:

I can relax and and be myself.

Word of the Day: Accurate- Correct, Exact, Precise

_____

_____

_____

_____

_____

_____

"My Feelings Matter"

 **SPEAK FREELY**

Date:

Today I am grateful for:

_____

_____

Best Moment of my Day:

_____

_____

Happiness Scale

☆ ☆ ☆ ☆ ☆

Affirmation of the Day:
I have so much to be grateful for!

 # "My Feelings Matter"

_____

_____

_____

_____

_____

_____

_____

Word of the Day: Pride-
Feeling of self-worth in oneself; Self-esteem.

 **SPEAK FREELY**

Date:

Today I am grateful for:

_____

_____

Best Moment of my Day:

_____

_____

Happiness Scale

☆ ☆ ☆ ☆ ☆

Affirmation of the Day:
I can turn a bad situation around!

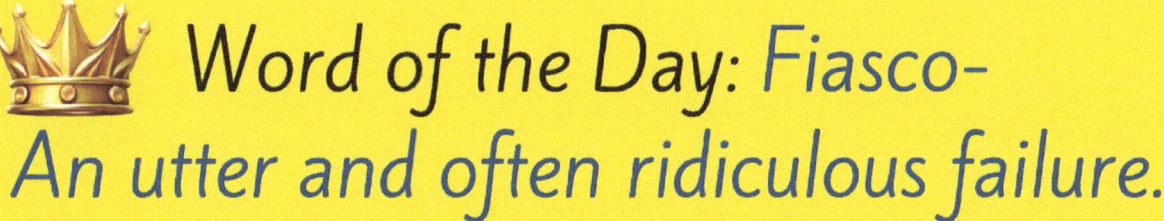 **Word of the Day: Fiasco-**
An utter and often ridiculous failure.

_____

_____

_____

_____

_____

_____

"My Feelings Matter"

 **SPEAK FREELY**

Date:

Today I am grateful for:

_____

_____

Best Moment of my Day:

_____

_____

Happiness Scale

☆ ☆ ☆ ☆ ☆

Affirmation of the Day:

I am capable!

"My Feelings Matter"

_____

_____

_____

_____

_____

_____

_____

**Word of the Day: Apathy-
Lack of emotion or lack of interest.**

 **SPEAK FREELY**

Date:

Today I am grateful for:

_____

_____

Best Moment of my Day:

_____

_____

Happiness Scale

☆ ☆ ☆ ☆ ☆

Affirmation of the Day:

I have a great personality!

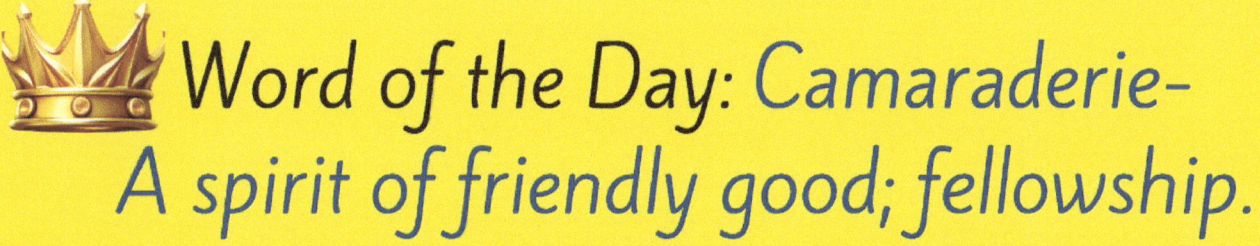 **Word of the Day:** *Camaraderie-*
A spirit of friendly good; fellowship.

_____

_____

_____

_____

_____

_____

"My Feelings Matter"

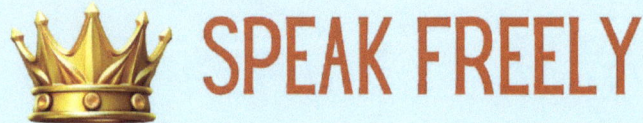 **SPEAK FREELY**

 Date:

Today I am grateful for:

_____

_____

Best Moment of my Day:

_____

_____

Happiness Scale

☆ ☆ ☆ ☆ ☆

Affirmation of the Day:

I am loved for who I am!

"My Feelings Matter"

_____

_____

_____

_____

_____

_____

_____

Word of the Day: Accumulate-
Gather together or acquire an increasing number.

 **SPEAK FREELY**

Date:

Today I am grateful for:

_____

_____

Best Moment of my Day:

_____

_____

Happiness Scale

☆ ☆ ☆ ☆ ☆

Affirmation of the Day:
I am a good person.

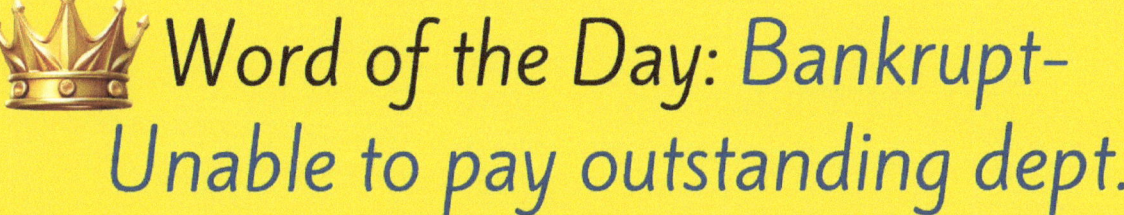 **Word of the Day:** Bankrupt- Unable to pay outstanding dept.

_____

_____

_____

_____

_____

_____

_____

"My Feelings Matter"

 **SPEAK FREELY**

Date:

Today I am grateful for:

_____

_____

Best Moment of my Day:

_____

_____

Happiness Scale

☆ ☆ ☆ ☆ ☆

Affirmation of the Day:

When I mess up, I can try again!

 # "My Feelings Matter"

_____

_____

_____

_____

_____

_____

_____

Word of the Day: Tax- Contribution to the state revenue by the government on workers income, or goods purchased.

 **SPEAK FREELY**

Date:

Today I am grateful for:

_____

_____

Best Moment of my Day:

_____

_____

Happiness Scale

☆ ☆ ☆ ☆ ☆

Affirmation of the Day:

I love me!

👑 **Word of the Day: Credit Score-**
A number indicating how likely someone will repay a loan. The higher, the better.

_____

_____

_____

_____

_____

_____

"My Feelings Matter"

 **SPEAK FREELY**

Date:

Today I am grateful for:

_____

_____

Best Moment of my Day:

_____

_____

Happiness Scale
☆ ☆ ☆ ☆ ☆

Affirmation of the Day:
I am patient and calm!

"My Feelings Matter"

_____

_____

_____

_____

_____

_____

Word of the Day: Abreast- Staying informed; Know all the most recent facts.

 **SPEAK FREELY**

Date:

Today I am grateful for:

_____

_____

Best Moment of my Day:

_____

_____

 Happiness Scale

☆ ☆ ☆ ☆ ☆

Affirmation of the Day:
I can do anything I put my mind too.

Word of the Day: *Solidarity-*
Unity between people; A group cohesive social bond.

_____

_____

_____

_____

_____

_____

_____

"My Feelings Matter"

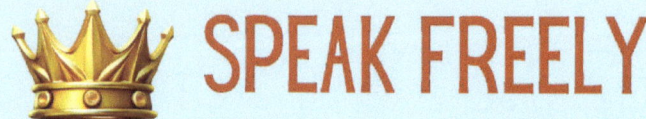 **SPEAK FREELY**

Date:

Today I am grateful for:

_____

_____

Best Moment of my Day:

_____

_____

Happiness Scale

☆ ☆ ☆ ☆ ☆

Affirmation of the Day:

I always do my best!

 # "My Feelings Matter"

_____

_____

_____

_____

_____

_____

_____

**Word of the Day: Cohesive-
Fit together well; work well together.**

 **SPEAK FREELY**

Date:

Today I am grateful for:

_____

_____

Best Moment of my Day:

_____

_____

Affirmation of the Day:
My opinions are valuable!

👑 **Word of the Day: Loitering-**
Standing around a place without a specific purpose.

_____

_____

_____

_____

_____

_____

_____

"My Feelings Matter"

 **SPEAK FREELY**

Date:

Today I am grateful for:

_____

_____

Best Moment of my Day:

_____

_____

Happiness Scale
☆ ☆ ☆ ☆ ☆

Affirmation of the Day:

My life is good!

 # "My Feelings Matter"

_____

_____

_____

_____

_____

_____

_____

Word of the Day: Cease- **Bring or come to an end.**

 **SPEAK FREELY**

Date:

Today I am grateful for:

_____

_____

Best Moment of my Day:

_____

_____

Happiness Scale

Affirmation of the Day:

I love to learn!

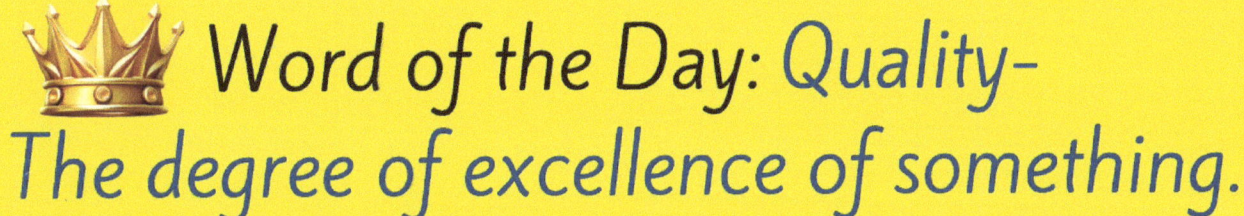 **Word of the Day:** *Quality-*
The degree of excellence of something.

_____

_____

_____

_____

_____

_____

_____

"My Feelings Matter"

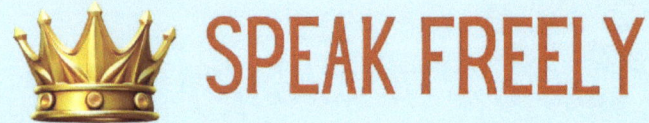 **SPEAK FREELY**

 Date:

Today I am grateful for:

_____

_____

Best Moment of my Day:

_____

_____

 Happiness Scale

☆ ☆ ☆ ☆ ☆

Affirmation of the Day:

I will succeed!

 # "My Feelings Matter"

_____

_____

_____

_____

_____

_____

_____

Word of the Day: Persistent-
Continuing to do something, although it's hard.
Not quitting.

 **SPEAK FREELY**

Date:

Today I am grateful for:

_____

_____

Best Moment of my Day:

_____

_____

Happiness Scale

Affirmation of the Day:

I am creative!

👑 **Word of the Day:** *Flabbergasted- Feel intense shock, surprise, or wonder.*

_____

_____

_____

_____

_____

_____

_____

"My Feelings Matter"

 **SPEAK FREELY**

Date:

Today I am grateful for:

_____

_____

Best Moment of my Day:

_____

_____

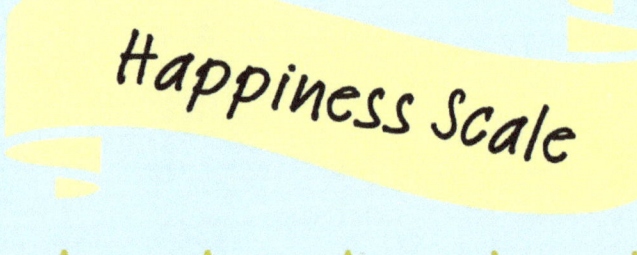
Happiness Scale

Affirmation of the Day:
It's OK to be different!

"My Feelings Matter"

_____

_____

_____

_____

_____

_____

_____

Word of the Day: Nonchalant- A person's behavior that is casually calm and relaxed.

 **SPEAK FREELY**

Date:

Today I am grateful for:

_____

_____

Best Moment of my Day:

_____

_____

Happiness Scale

☆ ☆ ☆ ☆ ☆

Affirmation of the Day:
My spirit is powerful!

 **Word of the Day:** *Flatulence- Excessive farting.*

_____

_____

_____

_____

_____

_____

_____

"My Feelings Matter"

 **SPEAK FREELY**

Date:

Today I am grateful for:

_____

_____

Best Moment of my Day:

_____

_____

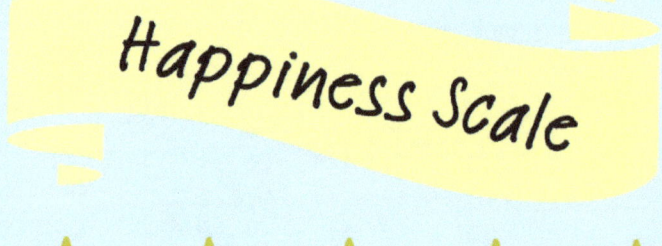 Happiness Scale

Affirmation of the Day:

My light shines bright!

"My Feelings Matter"

_____

_____

_____

_____

_____

_____

_____

Word of the Day: Plethora- *Excessive quantity or fullness.*

 **SPEAK FREELY** Date:

Today I am grateful for:

_____

_____

Best Moment of my Day:

_____

_____

 Happiness Scale

Affirmation of the Day:

I believe in my dreams!

Word of the Day: Acclimate-
Adapt to a new temperature, altitude, climate, environment, or situation.

_____

_____

_____

_____

_____

_____

_____

"My Feelings Matter"

 **SPEAK FREELY**

Date:

Today I am grateful for:

_____

_____

Best Moment of my Day:

_____

_____

Happiness Scale

☆ ☆ ☆ ☆ ☆

Affirmation of the Day:
I am a good listener!

 # "My Feelings Matter"

_____

_____

_____

_____

_____

_____

_____

Word of the Day: Dubious-
Feeling unsure or uncertain about something.

 **SPEAK FREELY**

Date:

Today I am grateful for:

_____

_____

Best Moment of my Day:

_____

_____

Happiness Scale

☆ ☆ ☆ ☆ ☆

Affirmation of the Day:
I have alot to offer!

Word of the Day: Inherit.
To receive property, a right, or a title, from someone after they pass away.

"My Feelings Matter"

 **SPEAK FREELY**

Date:

Today I am grateful for:

_____

_____

Best Moment of my Day:

_____

_____

Happiness Scale

☆ ☆ ☆ ☆ ☆

Affirmation of the Day:

I am proud of myself!

"My Feelings Matter"

_____

_____

_____

_____

_____

_____

_____

Word of the Day: Discretion-
Power of being careful with what one does.
Showing discernment or good judgement.

 **SPEAK FREELY**

Date:

Today I am grateful for:

_____

_____

Best Moment of my Day:

_____

_____

Happiness Scale

Affirmation of the Day:

I love who I am!

Word of the Day: Discernment-
The ability to understand, perceive, and judge things clearly.

_____

_____

_____

_____

_____

_____

_____

"My Feelings Matter"

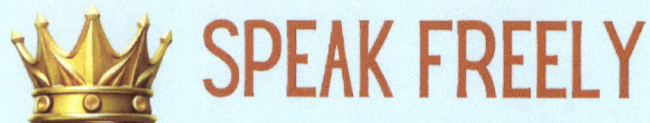 **SPEAK FREELY**

Date:

Today I am grateful for:

_____

_____

Best Moment of my Day:

_____

_____

Happiness Scale

☆ ☆ ☆ ☆ ☆

Affirmation of the Day:
I love making new friends!

"My Feelings Matter"

_____

_____

_____

_____

_____

_____

_____

_____

Word of the Day: Loyalty-
Quality of being faithful to commitments or obligations.

 **SPEAK FREELY**

 Date:

Today I am grateful for:

_____

_____

Best Moment of my Day:

_____

_____

_____

Happiness Scale

Affirmation of the Day:
I can advocate for myself!

Word of the Day: Humble-
Does not believe they are better than everyone else.

_____

_____

_____

_____

_____

_____

_____

"My Feelings Matter"

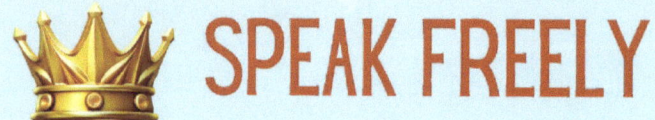 **SPEAK FREELY**

Date:

Today I am grateful for:

_____

_____

Best Moment of my Day:

_____

_____

Happiness Scale

Affirmation of the Day:
I will do great things!

 # "My Feelings Matter"

___

___

___

___

___

___

___

Word of the Day: Analogy– Comparison between two things that are otherwise different, based on a resemblance.

 **SPEAK FREELY**

Date:

Today I am grateful for:

_____

_____

Best Moment of my Day:

_____

_____

Happiness Scale

☆ ☆ ☆ ☆ ☆

Affirmation of the Day:
Learning from my mistakes help me grow!

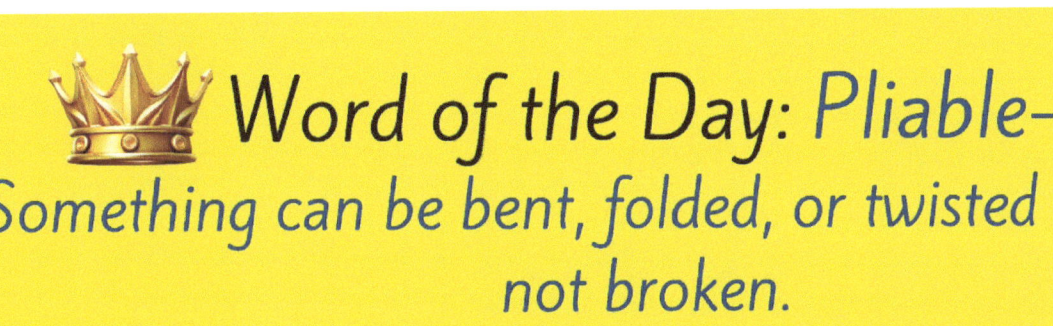 **Word of the Day: Pliable-** Something can be bent, folded, or twisted easily, but not broken.

_____
_____
_____
_____
_____
_____
_____

"My Feelings Matter"

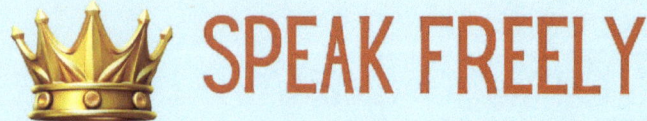 # SPEAK FREELY

Date:

Today I am grateful for:

_____

_____

Best Moment of my Day:

_____

_____

Happiness Scale

☆ ☆ ☆ ☆ ☆

Affirmation of the Day:

I am strong inside and out!

"My Feelings Matter"

_____

_____

_____

_____

_____

_____

_____

Word of the Day: Potential-
Having or showing the capacity to become or develop into something in the future.

 **SPEAK FREELY**

Date:

Today I am grateful for:

_____

_____

Best Moment of my Day:

_____

_____

 Happiness Scale

☆ ☆ ☆ ☆ ☆

Affirmation of the Day:
I can choose my friends!

👑 **Word of the Day: Influence-** *Indirectly affect or change someone or something.*

_____

_____

_____

_____

_____

_____

"My Feelings Matter"

 **SPEAK FREELY**

Date:

Today I am grateful for:

_____

_____

Best Moment of my Day:

_____

_____

Happiness Scale

☆ ☆ ☆ ☆ ☆

Affirmation of the Day:
I am not alone!

"My Feelings Matter"

_____

_____

_____

_____

_____

_____

_____

Word of the Day: Career-
A profession someone does for a long time.

 **SPEAK FREELY**

Date:

Today I am grateful for:

_____

_____

Best Moment of my Day:

_____

_____

 Happiness Scale

Affirmation of the Day:
I look my best everyday!

Word of the Day: Passion-
Strong feeling of enthusiasm or excitement about doing something.

_____

_____

_____

_____

_____

_____

"My Feelings Matter"

 **SPEAK FREELY**

 Date:

Today I am grateful for:

_____

_____

Best Moment of my Day:

_____

_____

_____

 Happiness Scale

☆ ☆ ☆ ☆ ☆

Affirmation of the Day:

I am safe!

"My Feelings Matter"

_____

_____

_____

_____

_____

_____

_____

Word of the Day: Obstacle- *Something that makes it difficult to do something else.*

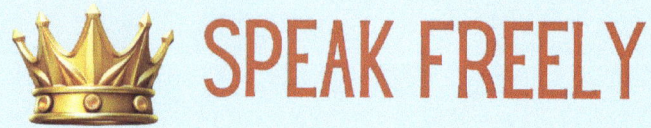 **SPEAK FREELY**

Date:

Today I am grateful for:

_____

_____

Best Moment of my Day:

_____

_____

 Happiness Scale

☆ ☆ ☆ ☆ ☆

Affirmation of the Day:

I choose peace!

 **Word of the Day: Remiss-** Careless or inattentive.

_____

_____

_____

_____

_____

_____

"My Feelings Matter"

 **SPEAK FREELY**

Date:

Today I am grateful for:

_____

_____

Best Moment of my Day:

_____

_____

_____

Happiness Scale

Affirmation of the Day:

I am a King!

"My Feelings Matter"

_____

_____

_____

_____

_____

_____

_____

Word of the Day: Investment- Committing money to receive more money later.

 **SPEAK FREELY**

Date:

Today I am grateful for:

_____

_____

Best Moment of my Day:

_____

_____

Happiness Scale

☆ ☆ ☆ ☆ ☆

Affirmation of the Day:
Self-love is important!

 **Word of the Day: Copiously-** In a large quantity.

_____

_____

_____

_____

_____

_____

_____

"My Feelings Matter"

Dear Young King,

This is only the beginning to finding your pathway in life. Your feelings Matter! Writing provides strength and allots for growth.

While you are living in a world that will never love you back, remember, Knowledge is power, stay focused, and self-love is the best love one can have.

Author Michelle Knight

www.bmrbookcase.com
1024 Centerbrooke Ln Ste. F 163
Suffulk, VA, 23434

www.ingramcontent.com/pod-product-compliance
Lightning Source LLC
Chambersburg PA
CBHW041407010526
44107CB00015B/1106